Learn About

THE FIVE SENSES

Seeing

by Susan B. Katz

Children's Press®
An imprint of Scholastic Inc.

Special thanks to our consultant Dr. Ron Spalter, OD, for his insight on sight!

Special thanks also to our medical content consultant, An Huang, MD, PhD, professor of physiology, New York Medical College.

Library of Congress Cataloging-in-Publication Data
Names: Katz, Susan B., 1971– author.
Title: Seeing / by Susan B. Katz.
Description: First edition. | New York, NY: Children's Press, an imprint of Scholastic Inc., [2023] | Series: Learn about: the five senses | Includes index. | Audience: Ages 5–7. | Audience: Grades K–1. | Summary: "How do we experience the world? Let's learn all about the five senses! The sense of sight is one of our five senses. And it is amazing! Among many other things, it helps us see where we are going, recognize our family and friends, and learn in school. Learn about seeing, how it works, and common problems and diseases connected with it, with this perfect first introduction to the sense of sight! ABOUT THE SERIES: The human body is amazing! It gives us five different ways to learn about the world around us: through the eyes, through the skin, through the tongue, through the ears, and through the nose. Thanks to these parts of our bodies, we can see, feel, taste, hear, and smell. These are the five senses! Why do bananas taste so good? Why does tickling cause so much laughter? Illustrated with familiar examples, this fun nonfiction set in the Learn About series gives readers a close-up look at the five senses, and it teaches them how each of the senses work."— Provided by publisher.
Identifiers: LCCN 2022056747 (print) | LCCN 2022056748 (ebook) | ISBN 9781338898231 (library binding) | ISBN 9781338898248 (paperback) | ISBN 9781338898255 (ebk)
Subjects: LCSH: Vision—Juvenile literature. | Eye—Juvenile literature. | Senses and sensation—Juvenile literature. | BISAC: JUVENILE NONFICTION / Concepts / Senses & Sensation | JUVENILE NONFICTION / General
Classification: LCC QP475.7 .K38 2023 (print) | LCC QP475.7 (ebook) | DDC 612.8/4—dc23/eng/20230124
LC record available at https://lccn.loc.gov/2022056747
LC ebook record available at https://lccn.loc.gov/2022056748

Copyright © 2024 by Scholastic Inc.

All rights reserved. Published by Children's Press, an imprint of Scholastic Inc., *Publishers since 1920.* SCHOLASTIC, CHILDREN'S PRESS, and associated logos are trademarks and/or registered trademarks of Scholastic Inc.

The publisher does not have any control over and does not assume any responsibility for author or third-party websites or their content.

No part of this publication may be reproduced, stored in a retrieval system, or transmitted in any form or by any means, electronic, mechanical, photocopying, recording, or otherwise, without written permission of the publisher. For information regarding permission, write to Scholastic Inc., Attention: Permissions Department, 557 Broadway, New York, NY 10012.

10 9 8 7 6 5 4 3 2 1   24 25 26 27 28

Printed in China, 62
First edition, 2024

Book design by Kathleen Petelinsek

Photos ©: 4–5: Wavebreakmedia/Getty Images; 7: sam74100/Getty Images; 9 left: Bozena_Fulawka/Getty Images; 12 left: kiankhoon/Getty Images; 12 right: 8 baona/Getty Images; 13 left: Jon Feingersh Photography Inc/Getty Images; 14–15: Olga Mosman/Getty Images; 19 bottom: Teresa Short/Getty Images; 20: Instants/Getty Images; 21: andresr/Getty Images; 22: Tim UR/Getty Images; 24: Alika Obrazovskaya/Getty Images; 25: Scott T. Baxter/Getty Images; 28 bottom: Alongkot Sumritjearapol/Getty Images; 29 top: Martin Heyn/Getty Images; 29 center: Svetla Ilieva/EyeEm/Getty Images; 29 bottom: Andrey Zhuravlev/Getty Images; 30 top right: twinsterphoto/Getty Images; 30 center right: wundervisuals/Getty Images.

All other photos © Shutterstock.

TABLE OF CONTENTS

Keep Your Eye on the Ball! 4

Chapter 1: Eye Spy 6

Chapter 2: How Our Eyes Work 14

Chapter 3: Eye Problems 18

Activity: Guess the Objects 26

Animal Eyes 28

Protect Your Eyes! 30

Glossary 31

Index/About the Author 32

INTRODUCTION

Keep Your Eye on the Ball!

Have you ever played catch? In this game, you need to keep your eyes on the ball. That way you don't get hit, and you can catch it!

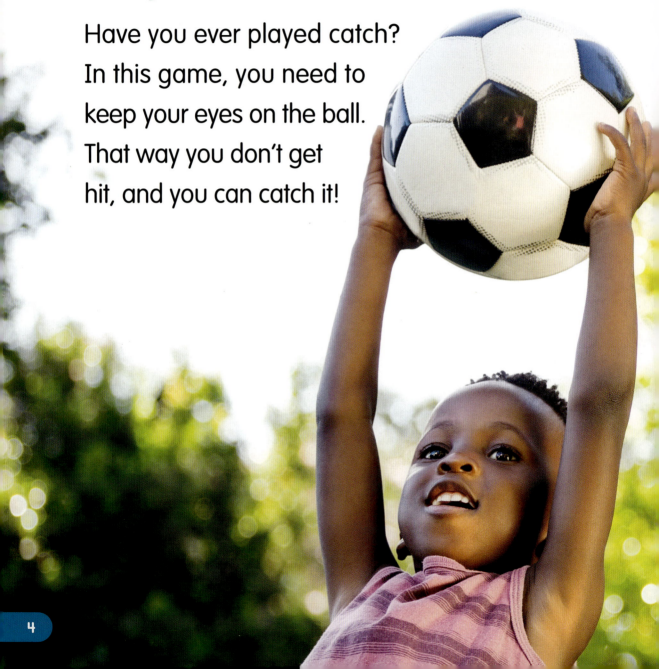

The main sense we use to play catch is sight. Sight is the ability to see. It is one of the five senses. The other four senses are hearing, smell, taste, and touch. They help us take in information about the world around us.

Most people use their sense of sight more than any other sense.

CHAPTER 1

Eye Spy

With our eyes, we can see where we are going when we walk or play. We recognize our family and friends. Our sight lets us read books and watch movies. It helps us learn in school.

Seeing keeps us safe so we don't fall. If we see danger, we can move away.

The average person will see 24 million images in their lifetime.

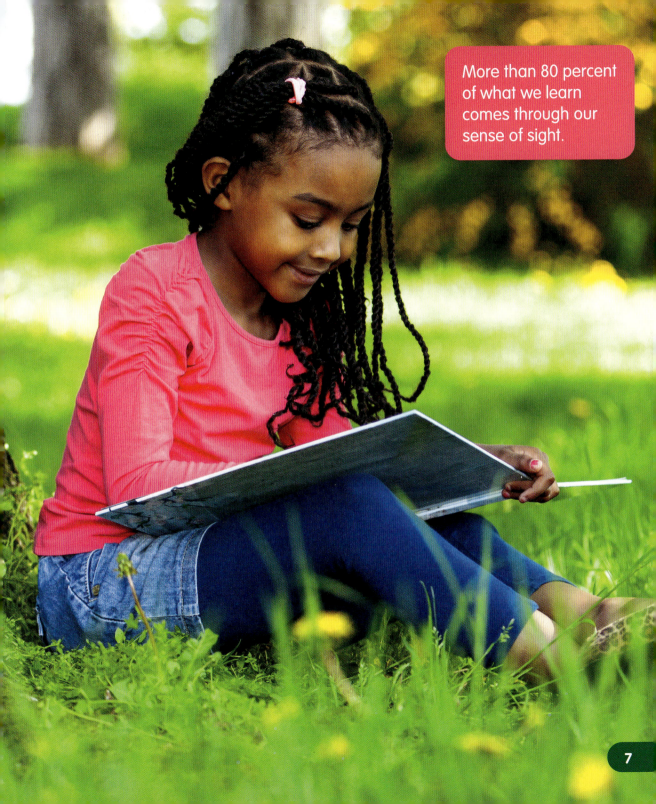

More than 80 percent of what we learn comes through our sense of sight.

Light **reflects** off objects around us. Then the light makes its way into our eyes. When light hits our eyes, we see color.

Our eyes really see only three colors: red, blue, and green. Every other color we see is a combination of these three.

Most people can see the red petals of a rose. They can see the colorful feathers of a parrot.

We can also see shapes. Our sense of sight tells us that a pumpkin is round. It tells us that a stop sign has eight sides.

When people, houses, or cars are far away, they look smaller to us.

The sense of sight also helps us judge how far away or close something is. That is called **depth perception**. We make decisions all the time using depth perception. Is that car far enough away to safely cross the street? How close is the store I want to enter?

Our eyes take in images around us and send information to our brain.

Our eyes can usually see many things without help. But, sometimes, we want to see things our eyes cannot see very well. These tools can help us!

TELESCOPE: We look through a telescope to see objects that are far off in the distance. We need it to see the stars, the moon, or other planets.

BINOCULARS: We can look through binoculars to see objects that are far away. Binoculars make them look a bit closer. We can use them to watch birds, whales, or an actor in a play.

Telescope

Binoculars

MICROSCOPE: It allows us to see very little bugs or cells. Things under the microscope look much, much bigger!

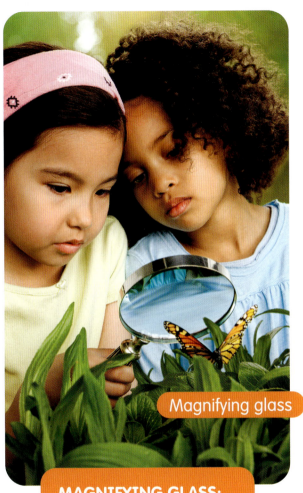

Magnifying glass

MAGNIFYING GLASS: This tool lets us see details up close, like the wings of a butterfly or very small print.

Microscope

CHAPTER 2

How Our Eyes Work

The human eye is an **organ** in our body. It has many parts. Some parts help us see. Some parts protect our eyes.

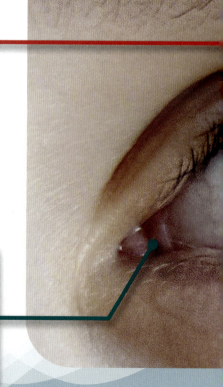

TEAR GLAND: Located under the skin, this is where tears are produced. Tears protect our eyes. They keep them clean and give them oxygen and water.

When we are really sad or very happy, our eyes might let out tears.

TEAR DUCT: Tears drain into the tear duct. These are the little holes in the corner of the eye. When we blink, tears spread on the eyelid.

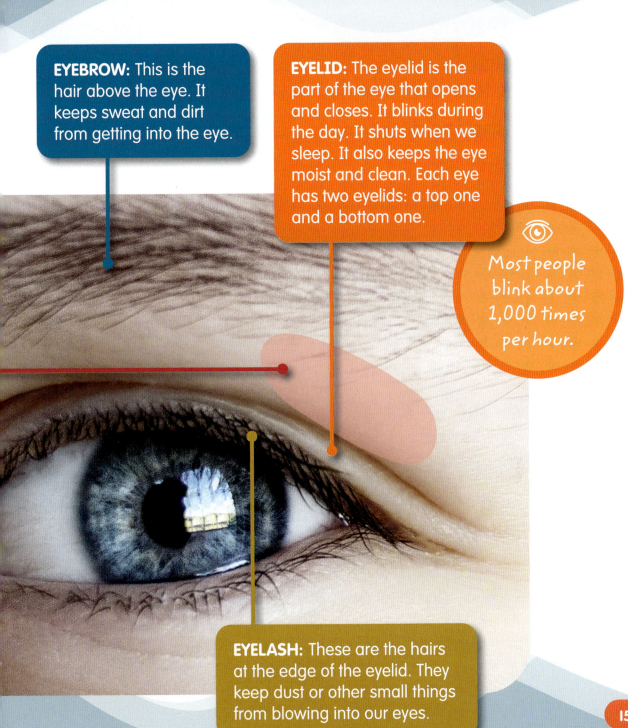

EYEBROW: This is the hair above the eye. It keeps sweat and dirt from getting into the eye.

EYELID: The eyelid is the part of the eye that opens and closes. It blinks during the day. It shuts when we sleep. It also keeps the eye moist and clean. Each eye has two eyelids: a top one and a bottom one.

Most people blink about 1,000 times per hour.

EYELASH: These are the hairs at the edge of the eyelid. They keep dust or other small things from blowing into our eyes.

Check this out! This is what the inside of our eye looks like.

CORNEA: This is the clear layer at the front of the eye. It protects the eye and helps it **focus**.

About three out of four people have brown eyes.

SCLERA: It is the white outer layer of the eye.

IRIS: The iris controls how much light the pupil lets in. It also gives the eye its color.

PUPIL: It is the black hole at the center of the iris. When it is dark outside, it opens to let as much light as possible into the eye. When there is light outside, it gets smaller to allow less light into the eye.

LENS: The lens is behind the pupil. It focuses the light coming through the pupil onto the retina. It allows us to see clearly.

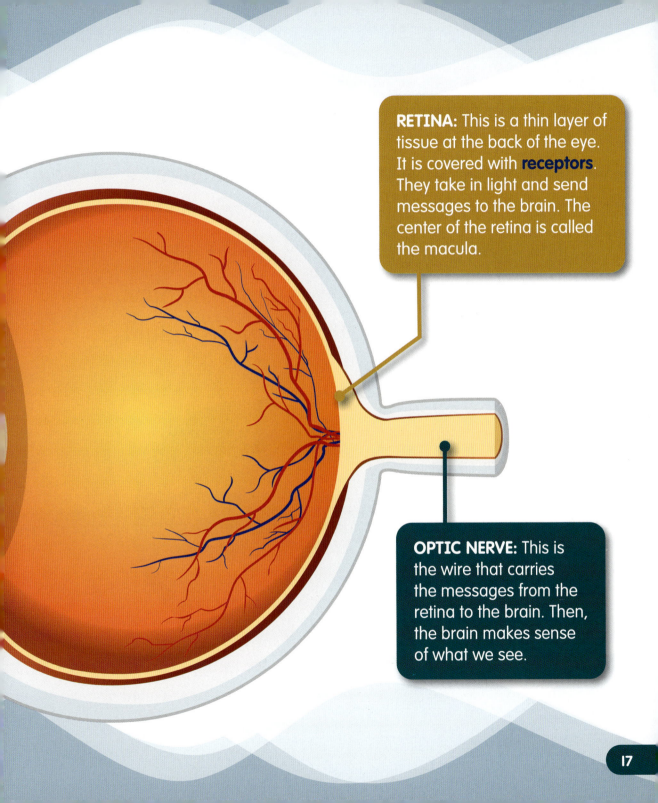

CHAPTER 3

Eye Problems

Sometimes our eyes can get infected. We can get a stye in our eye. It is a little bump on the eyelid that can hurt a bit. Or we might get pink eye. It makes our eyes really red and itchy. Then we might go to an eye doctor.

Pink eye can spread very easily. If you ever have it, do not touch your eyes and make sure to wash your hands often.

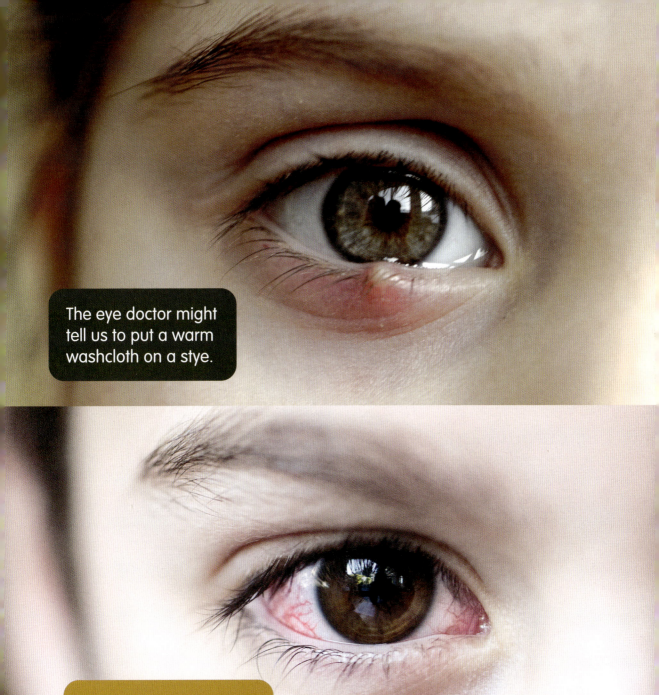

The eye doctor might tell us to put a warm washcloth on a stye.

Special eye drops can help our eyes heal when we have pink eye.

Sometimes things look blurry to certain people. The eye doctor does an exam to test our **vision**. The doctor can tell if we need glasses or contact lenses to see clearly. Do you wear glasses? One in every four kids in the world needs glasses or contact lenses!

An eye doctor might have us read letters and numbers from a chart like this one.

The eye doctor uses this special machine to examine your eyes.

Nearsighted (NEER-sye-tid) people are only able to see objects clearly if they are close to their eyes. It is a very common condition.

21

Color deficient people may not see the red on the top half of the apple. To them, it may look green, like the bottom half.

Some people are color **deficient**, also called color-blind. That means they cannot see the difference between certain colors. They cannot tell red and green apart. Or they cannot tell blue and yellow apart. Some other people can see things only in black and white, or in shades of gray.

Many more men than women are color deficient.

Some people are unable to see. They are called vision **impaired**, or blind. They might use a cane or a dog trained to help them get around. Blind people often have heightened, or stronger, senses of hearing, smell, and touch.

Guide dogs are trained to help people who have lost their sense of sight.

Vision impaired people might read books using raised bumps called Braille. They can feel the letters.

Together with the other senses, the sense of sight keeps us connected with the world around us. The five senses are amazing! What will your senses help you do today?

ACTIVITY: GUESS THE OBJECTS

Without using your sense of sight, guess what things are by only touching, smelling, or hearing them.

YOU WILL NEED:

- A bandana to use as a blindfold
- Common objects such as a pencil, a book, utensils, or a piece of fruit
- An adult to help you so you don't get hurt (or peek!)

STEPS:

1. Have an adult tie a blindfold around your eyes with the bandana.
2. Ask them to take out some common objects and place them on a tray.
3. One by one, feel each object. Smell it. See if it makes any noise. Guess what each object is without looking at it.
4. Tell the adult what you think each object is. Ask them to write down your guesses.
5. Untie the blindfold and see if your guesses were right.

WHAT HAPPENED?

When you were doing the guessing activity, you probably used your senses of hearing, smell, and touch more than you usually do. When you can't see, your other senses heighten, or get stronger.

ANIMAL EYES

Amazing Night Vision
Tiger eyes have large lenses and pupils. This lets in more light from outside. They also have special retinas that are able to capture light when it is dark outside. A tiger's night vision is about six times better than that of a human!

Fixed Eyes
Owls, like humans, have two eyes in the front of their head. But their eyes can't move side to side as ours do. They are fixed. This is why they have to turn their heads around instead! Owls also have the best night vision in the animal kingdom!

Eyes All Around
Almost all spiders have eight eyes. They use their front eyes to hunt. They use their side eyes to detect movement. Their eight eyes keep them safe! Like owls, spiders' eyes are fixed.

Eyes That Don't Blink
Lots of sharks don't blink. They close their eyelids only when they need to protect their eyes. This happens very rarely. Some sharks don't even have eyelids at all! Shark corneas are a lot like our corneas. They have been put into humans with vision problems.

Three Eyelids
Camels live in the desert. They have huge eyes on the sides of their head. To protect them from blowing sand, camels have three eyelids instead of two. They also have two rows of long eyelashes to keep sand out.

Vertical Pupils
Most animals have round pupils. But cats' pupils are vertical. It lets them see in low light. It also helps them judge how far away objects are. Then they can pounce on a mouse or a cat toy!

PROTECT YOUR EYES!

It is important to take care of our eyes! We can use a variety of glasses and goggles to protect them in different situations.

Scientists and construction workers use safety goggles.

We use goggles when we swim to see underwater.

Sunglasses block out strong rays from the sun.

If you wear glasses, make sure to take good care of them.

Ski goggles block out sunrays and also keep our eyes warm in cold weather.

GLOSSARY

Braille (BRAYL) a system of writing and printing for blind people that uses raised dots for letters and numbers

deficient (di-FISH-uhnt) lacking something necessary

depth perception (DEPTH pur-SEP-shuhn) what allows us to tell how far away or close up something is

focus (FOH-kuhs) to adjust the eyes to see something clearly

impaired (im-PAIRD) something damaged that is less effective

organ (OR-guhn) a part of the body, such as the heart or the eyes, that has a certain purpose

receptors (ri-SEP-turz) nerve endings that sense stimulus, such as pressure, touch, heat, or light

reflects (ri-FLEKS) throws back heat, light, or sound from a surface

vision (VIZH-uhn) the sense of sight

INDEX

animals, 28–29
blindness, 24–25
blinking, 15
Braille, 25
color of eyes, 16
colors, seeing, 8–9, 22–23
deficient, color, 22–23
depth perception, 11
distance, 10–11, 21

eyes
  parts of, 14–17
  problems with, 18–25
  protecting, 30
focusing, 16
impaired, vision, 24–25
nearsightedness, 21
organs, 14
pink eye, 18–19

receptors, 17
reflected light, 8
styes, 18–19
tears, 14
vision (sight)
  defined, 5
  learning through, 6–7
  tools to help, 12–13
  use of, 4–5, 26–27
vision tests, 20–21

ABOUT THE AUTHOR

Susan B. Katz loves color in nature. She has been wearing glasses or contacts for the better part of 40 years, and her grandfather, brother, and nephew are all color deficient! Susan is the bestselling, award-winning, Spanish bilingual author of over 50 books. Check out her books at www.SusanKatzBooks.com. She is also a wildlife photographer! You can see her photos at behance.net/susanbkatz.